World of Reptiles

Chameleons

by Jason Glaser

Consultants:
The Staff of Reptile Gardens
Rapid City, South Dakota

Capstone
press

Mankato, Minnesota

Bridgestone Books are published by Capstone Press,
151 Good Counsel Drive, P.O. Box 669, Mankato, Minnesota 56002.
www.capstonepress.com

Library of Congress Cataloging-in-Publication Data
Glaser, Jason.
    Chameleons / by Jason Glaser.
      p. cm.—(Bridgestone books. World of reptiles)
    Summary: "A brief introduction to chameleons, discussing their characteristics, range,
habitat, food, offspring, and dangers. Includes a range map, life cycle diagram, and amazing
facts"—Provided by publisher.
    Includes bibliographical references and index.
    ISBN-13: 978-0-7368-5420-7 (hardcover)
    ISBN-10: 0-7368-5420-7 (hardcover)
    1. Chameleons—Juvenile literature. I. Title. II. Series: Bridgestone books. World of reptiles.
QL666.L23G53 2006
597.95'6—dc22   2005015592

Editorial Credits

Jennifer Besel, editor; Enoch Peterson, set designer; Kim Brown and Patrick Dentinger, book
    designers; Jo Miller, photo researcher; Scott Thoms, photo editor; Tami Collins, illustrator;
    Nancy Steers, map illustrator

Photo Credits

Allen Blake Sheldon, 16
Corbis/Tom Brakefield, 10
Digital Vision, 1
Dwight R. Kuhn, 20
Getty Images Inc./The Image Bank/Bob Elsdale, 12
NHPA/Anthony Bannister, 18
Pete Carmichael, 4
Seapics.com/Kevin Schafer, cover
Visuals Unlimited/ Tom J. Ulrich, 6

1 2 3 4 5 6 11 10 09 08 07 06

Table of Contents

Chameleons

High in a tree, a chameleon spots a bird coming near. The chameleon's body quickly turns from green to black. It is telling the bird to go away.

Chameleons are reptiles that are known for their ability to change colors. Chameleons don't change colors to blend in with their surroundings. They change colors to communicate. Chameleons also change colors to soak up heat from the sun. Like all reptiles, chameleons are **cold-blooded**. They need to keep their bodies warm.

◀ When a chameleon is frightened, its entire body changes color in a matter of seconds.

What Chameleons Look Like

A chameleon's body is made for living in trees. Chameleon feet are shaped like **pincers** to grab branches, and their long tails help them balance when it's windy. Chameleons are normally green, gray, or brown. These colors blend in with a tree's leaves and twigs.

Chameleons are covered with scales. Under the scales are layers of different colored skin cells. These cells change size when a chameleon changes color. Some cells grow larger, blocking the color from other cells. The chameleon turns the color of the large cells.

◄ A chameleon's natural body color blends in with leaves and branches to protect it from danger.

Chameleon Range Map

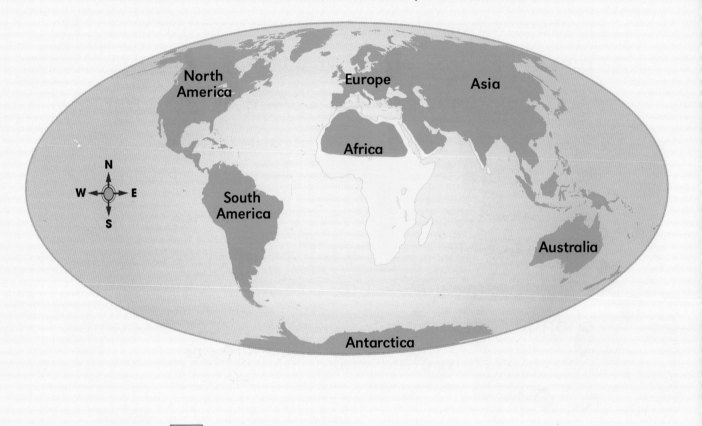

Where Chameleons Live

Chameleons in the World

Most of the world's chameleons live on the African island of Madagascar. Chameleons also live on Africa's mainland and in southern Asia, Europe, and the Middle East.

Many chameleons also live in Hawaii. These lizards have not always lived on the islands. In the 1970s, people brought chameleons to Hawaii to have as pets. Many chameleons were let go in the wild. With no **predators** to eat them, chameleons spread throughout Hawaii.

Chameleon Habitats

Chameleons live in many habitats. Most chameleons live in warm, wet rain forests. Other chameleons make their homes in hot, dry deserts. A few chameleons even live high in the mountains.

Chameleons spend most of their lives in trees. They are good climbers, and they can easily hide in leaves and branches. Most chameleons don't spend much time on the ground. On the ground, these slow movers are easy **prey** for predators.

◀ Chameleons stay hidden high in the trees because on the ground they move less than 20 feet (6 meters) a minute.

What Chameleons Eat

Chameleons spend most of their time hunting for food. They catch insects with their long, sticky tongues. Some chameleons even eat small lizards and birds.

Chameleons don't have to move much to spot prey. A chameleon's eyes can move in two different directions at the same time. The chameleon can look up with one eye and forward with the other. When the chameleon sees prey, it turns slowly toward it. Then it shoots out its sticky tongue to grab its food.

◄ A chameleon can shoot its tongue out of its mouth at speeds of up to 13 miles (21 kilometers) per hour.

The Life Cycle of a Chameleon

Egg

Hatchling

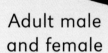
Adult male
and female

Adolescent
chameleon

Producing Young

Chameleons change colors when they are ready to **mate**. Male chameleons watch the females' colors. Pale colors let the male know he is allowed to come near.

After mating, most females lay eggs in a nest in the ground. A female may lay up to 50 eggs. She covers her eggs with dirt to hide them from predators.

A few types of chameleons don't lay eggs. Some females carry eggs inside their bodies. They carry the eggs until the babies are ready to be born.

Growing Up

After a few months, baby chameleons are ready to be born. Babies hatch from their eggs in the dirt and struggle to the surface. Baby chameleons leave the nest as soon as they hatch.

Females that carry eggs in their bodies give birth to live young. These females don't dig nests in the ground. They give birth on tree branches.

All baby chameleons take care of themselves as soon as they are born. They use their tongues to catch flies, gnats, and butterflies.

◀ At birth, baby chameleons are no larger than an adult's fingernail.

Dangers to Chameleons

Chameleons can't defend themselves very well. They often become meals for hungry predators. Hawks, owls, and other birds eat chameleons. Small chameleons are eaten by snakes and even spiders.

People are also a threat to chameleons. Many chameleons are kept as pets. But chameleons are hard to care for. They die quickly in **captivity**.

People also destroy chameleons' habitats. In Africa, forests where chameleons live are being cut down. Some countries have created parks to protect these colorful lizards.

◄ Chameleons have the poorest hearing of all lizards, so they can't hear predators coming.

Amazing Facts about Chameleons

- Chameleons can't hear or smell very well. They have to use their great eyesight to protect themselves.
- Unlike most reptiles, chameleons chew their prey. The chameleon begins chewing as soon as its tongue is back in its mouth, even if it missed its target.
- A chameleon's tongue can catch and pull in prey that weighs up to half of the chameleon's own body weight.
- Chameleons live alone. They will hiss at and chase away other chameleons.

◄ To search for prey and predators, a chameleon looks up, down, and behind without ever moving its head.

Glossary

captivity (kap-TIH-vuh-tee)—an environment that is not a natural habitat

cold-blooded (KOHLD-BLUHD-id)—having a body temperature that is the same as the surroundings; all reptiles are cold-blooded.

mate (MAYT)—to join together to produce young

pincer (PIN-sur)—an object with two parts that pinch or grab

predator (PRED-uh-tur)—an animal that hunts other animals for food

prey (PRAY)—an animal hunted by another animal for food

Read More

Deiters, Erika, and Jim Deiters. *Chameleons*. Animals of the Rain Forest. Austin, Texas: Raintree Steck-Vaughn, 2002.

Miller, Jake. *The Chameleon*. The Lizard Library. New York: PowerKids Press, 2003.

Internet Sites

FactHound offers a safe, fun way to find Internet sites related to this book. All of the sites on FactHound have been researched by our staff.

Here's how:
1. Visit *www.facthound.com*
2. Type in this special code **0736854207** for age-appropriate sites. Or enter a search word related to this book for a more general search.
3. Click on the **Fetch It** button.

FactHound will fetch the best sites for you!

Index